21st Century Computer Solutions

A MANUAL ACCOUNTING SIMULATION

PATRICIA A. NG

authorHOUSE®

AuthorHouse™ LLC
1663 Liberty Drive
Bloomington, IN 47403
www.authorhouse.com
Phone: 1-800-839-8640

Published by AuthorHouse 07/18/2014

ISBN: 978-1-4969-2577-0 (sc)
ISBN: 978-1-4969-2578-7 (e)

Library of Congress Control Number: 2014912500

To James
for his quiet, patient and unfailing support
during the development of this resource.

To my students (my guinea pigs)
for their inspiration, suggestions, constructive criticism
and their desire to learn.

CONTENTS

INTRODUCTION

The accounting cycle is best learned by doing. Thus, the goal of this accounting simulation is to provide the student with a hands-on approach to learning the accounting cycle--from analyzing and journalizing transactions and events to financial statement preparation and end-of-period closing. If completed manually, this simulation may take 10 - 14 hours to complete. Alternatively, the student may use computerized accounting packages such as Simply Accounting by Sage, QuickBooks®, MYOB®, etc.

Background Information

21st Century Computer Solutions is a sole proprietorship business owned and operated by Will B. Rich. The company is a computer reseller providing technical, software tutorial and other support services to its customers. Since its inception three years ago, the company has grown in size and profitability. Its customer make-up, too, has changed from mostly home computer users to mostly businesses and other organizations. The staff includes Barry Poor, a full-time technician, and **you, a part-time bookkeeper cum office manager**. Operating from a leased bay at the local strip mall, its share of utility costs is billed regularly by mall management. Sales to home users are on cash basis while sales to businesses and other entities are on credit with terms of **2/10, n/30**. Similarly, **vendors' credit terms** are **2/10, n/30**.

Internal control procedures and accounting/other practices:

- The owner communicates his instructions through inter-office memoranda. Additionally, he reviews vendors' and company's sales invoices and other business documents before giving them to the bookkeeper for appropriate action.

- All disbursements are made by cheque except for small expenses which are paid with petty cash. When bills are due, cheques are issued and supporting documents are reviewed and cancelled by the owner when he signs the cheques.

- The owner, himself, deposits cash receipts. From the authenticated deposit slip he prepares a cash deposit sheet from where journal entries are prepared.

- Also, the owner prepares the bi-weekly payroll. (To keep details to the minimum, payroll taxes are ignored.)

- **Goods and Services Tax (GST) of 5% and Provincial Sales Tax (PST) of 7% are calculated on the price of the purchase**. A 7% PST rate was chosen to illustrate the accounting for PST and does not necessarily reflect the rate levied by the Canadian provinces except for

1

Alberta which levies no PST. The Atlantic provinces collect a combined GST and PST called Harmonized Sales Tax (HST). **Discounts for early payment do not apply to GST and PST.**

- **A GST Payable** account is credited for GST on sales and is debited for the GST input tax credit on purchases. Periodically, the company remits the excess of the payable over the input tax credit to the Canada Revenue Agency or applies for a GST refund if the total input tax credit exceeds the GST on sales.

- **Sales of goods and services for personal/business use are subject to PST while sales of goods for resale are PST exempt. Periodically, the company remits the PST collected from customers to the appropriate government authority.**

- **The PST paid on goods and services purchased for the company's use is added to the cost.**

Additional Information

The company's chart of accounts, loan payment schedule, post-closing trial balance, details of accounts receivable and accounts payable as of June 30, 20__and information on its customers, vendors and employees are presented in the following pages.

21ˢᵗ Century Computer Solutions	
Chart of Accounts	
Account Number	Account Title
1010	Cash in Bank
1030	Petty Cash
1050	Accounts Receivable
1060	Allowance for Doubtful Accounts
1110	Notes Receivable
1120	Inventory
1150	Computer Supplies
1190	Office Supplies
1210	Prepaid Insurance
1510	Office Furniture & Equipment
1520	Accumulated Depreciation – Office Furniture & Equipment
1560	Motor Vehicle
1570	Accumulated Depreciation – Motor Vehicle
2010	Accounts Payable
2110	GST Payable
2130	PST Payable
2150	Salaries Payable
2550	Development Bank Loan Payable
3010	Will B. Rich, Capital
3020	Will B. Rich, Drawing
4010	Computer Sales
4011	Sales Discounts
4050	Service Fees
5010	Purchases
5020	Purchase Returns and Allowances
5030	Purchase Discounts
5040	Transportation In
5605	Depreciation Expense – Office Furniture & Equipment
5611	Depreciation Expense – Motor Vehicle
5615	Delivery Expense
5617	Insurance Expense
5619	Interest Expense
5621	Salaries Expense
5629	Computer Supplies Expense
5630	Office Supplies Expense
5632	Bad Debt Expense
5633	Rent Expense
5635	Telephone Expense
5637	Utilities Expense
5640	Miscellaneous Expense
9999	Income Summary

Patricia A. Ng

<table>
<tr><td colspan="4" align="center">**21st Century Computer Solutions**
Post-Closing Trial Balance
June 30, 20____</td></tr>
<tr><td rowspan="2">Account Number</td><td rowspan="2">Account Title</td><td colspan="2" align="center">Account Balances</td></tr>
<tr><td>Debit</td><td>Credit</td></tr>
<tr><td>1010</td><td>Cash in Bank</td><td>$ 22,873.46</td><td></td></tr>
<tr><td>1030</td><td>Petty Cash</td><td>250.00</td><td></td></tr>
<tr><td>1050</td><td>Accounts Receivable</td><td>20,208.00</td><td></td></tr>
<tr><td>1060</td><td>Allowance for Doubtful Accounts</td><td></td><td>$ 101.00</td></tr>
<tr><td>1110</td><td>Notes Receivable</td><td></td><td></td></tr>
<tr><td>1120</td><td>Inventory</td><td>3,060.24</td><td></td></tr>
<tr><td>1150</td><td>Computer Supplies</td><td>749.00</td><td></td></tr>
<tr><td>1190</td><td>Office Supplies</td><td>625.00</td><td></td></tr>
<tr><td>1210</td><td>Prepaid Insurance</td><td>726.00</td><td></td></tr>
<tr><td>1510</td><td>Office Furniture & Equipment</td><td>19,650.25</td><td></td></tr>
<tr><td>1520</td><td>Accum. Depreciation-Office Furniture & Equipment</td><td></td><td>6,163.00</td></tr>
<tr><td>1560</td><td>Motor Vehicle</td><td>48,850.00</td><td></td></tr>
<tr><td>1570</td><td>Accum. Depreciation-Motor Vehicle</td><td></td><td>5,682.00</td></tr>
<tr><td>2010</td><td>Accounts Payable</td><td></td><td>15,955.00</td></tr>
<tr><td>2110</td><td>GST Payable</td><td></td><td>1,820.00</td></tr>
<tr><td>2130</td><td>PST Payable</td><td></td><td>2,989.00</td></tr>
<tr><td>2150</td><td>Salaries Payable</td><td></td><td>2,400.00</td></tr>
<tr><td>2550</td><td>Development Bank Loan Payable</td><td></td><td>10,150.25</td></tr>
<tr><td>3010</td><td>Will B. Rich, Capital</td><td></td><td>71,731.70</td></tr>
<tr><td></td><td></td><td>$116,991.95</td><td>$ 116,991.95</td></tr>
<tr><td></td><td></td><td></td><td></td></tr>
</table>

<table>
<tr><td colspan="6" align="center">**Details of Accounts Receivable, June 30, 20_____**</td></tr>
<tr><td>Name</td><td>Date</td><td>Invoice No.</td><td>Pretax Amount</td><td>GST & PST</td><td>Total Amount</td></tr>
<tr><td>Beautiful Smiles Denture Clinic</td><td>June 15,20__</td><td>100715</td><td>$ 4,241.07</td><td>$ 508.93</td><td>$ 4,750.00</td></tr>
<tr><td>Bountiful Farms</td><td>June 4, 20___</td><td>100710</td><td>1,892.86</td><td>227.14</td><td>2,120.00</td></tr>
<tr><td>Mount Rose School District</td><td>June 20, 20__</td><td>100717</td><td>11,908.93</td><td>1,429.07</td><td>13,338.00</td></tr>
<tr><td></td><td></td><td></td><td></td><td></td><td>$20,208.00</td></tr>
</table>

<table>
<tr><td colspan="6" align="center">**Details of Accounts Payable, June 30, 20____**</td></tr>
<tr><td>Name</td><td>Date</td><td>Invoice No.</td><td>Pretax Amount</td><td>GST</td><td>Total Amount</td></tr>
<tr><td>CompuResource, Inc.</td><td>June 27, 20__</td><td>141</td><td>$ 868.57</td><td>$ 43.43</td><td>$ 912.00</td></tr>
<tr><td>Computer Systems Corp.</td><td>June 27, 20__</td><td>20852</td><td>13,836.19</td><td>691.81</td><td>14,528.00</td></tr>
<tr><td>Software, Etcetera</td><td>June 20, 20__</td><td>10798</td><td>490.48</td><td>24.52</td><td>515.00</td></tr>
<tr><td></td><td></td><td></td><td></td><td></td><td>$15,955.00</td></tr>
</table>

Instructions

1. Analyze the transactions and events occurring in July 20____ and record them in the appropriate journals. Use the:

    a. Sales Journal to record credit sales

    b. Purchases Journal for purchases on account

    c. Cash Receipts Journal for payments on account received from customers and for cash sales.

    d. Cash Disbursements Journal for payments made to vendors and others for goods and services and for other purposes. Also, write a cheque for each disbursement and complete the cheque stub.

    e. General Journal for all other transactions and events.

2. On a daily basis, post entries

    a. Recorded in the General Journal (GJ).

    b. Affecting vendors recorded in the Purchases Journal (PJ) and Cash Disbursements Journal (CDJ) to the vendors' accounts in the Accounts Payable Subsidiary Ledger.

    c. Affecting customers recorded in the Sales Journal (SJ)and the Cash Receipts Journal (CRJ) to the customers' accounts in the Accounts Receivable Subsidiary Ledger

    d. Affecting **Other Accounts** in the Cash Disbursements Journal (CDJ) to the appropriate accounts in the General Ledger.

3. At the end of the month

    a. Foot and cross foot the special journals and post column totals, except for **Other Accounts** total, to the General Ledger.

    b. Prepare schedules of accounts receivable and accounts payable for July 31 and agree totals to the controlling accounts in the General Ledger.

    c. Prepare a bank reconciliation then journalize and post the reconciling item/s to bring the balance of the Cash account agree with the adjusted balance on the bank reconciliation. Refer to the loan payment schedule for information relating to the monthly bank loan payment. Use the Miscellaneous Account to record the bank service charge.

    d. Agree the balance on the last check stub to the Cash account balance.

    e. Complete the worksheet

    f. Journalize and post the adjusting entries

    g. Prepare the following financial statements
        -   Multiple-step Income Statement
        -   Statement of Changes in Owner's Equity
        -   Classified Balance Sheet.

    h. Journalize and post closing entries.

    i. Prepare a post-closing trial Balance.

Loan Payment Schedule

	21st Century Computer Solutions Development Bank Loan Loan Payment Schedule (Partial)			
Date	Payment	Principal	Interest	Ending Balance
01-Apr	$933.33	$851.93	$81.40	$11,864.41
01-May	933.33	854.23	79.10	11,010.18
01-Jun	933.33	859.93	73.40	10,150.25
01-Jul	933.33	865.66	67.67	9,284.59
Aug. 1	933.33	871.44	61.89	8,413.15

JULY TRANSACTIONS

July 3   Sold a Dell notebook computer to Lakeview University College.

---

*21*st CENTURY COMPUTER SOLUTIONS

231 Main Street, Red Deer
AB, T4N 1V6

SALES INVOICE
Invoice No. 100721
Date: July 3, 20___

Sold to: Lakeview University College
          101 Lake Drive
          Centralta, AB T4P 1N5

Customer PO: 101896
Shipped To: Same
Terms: 2/10, n/30

SYSTEM DESCRIPTION

Pentium 4 enhanced mobile performance internet ready system

Component	Component Description	Unit	System Price	Extended Price
Processor	Mobile Intel Pentium 4 processor @ 3.06GHz			
Display	15" SXGA+ TFT Display			
Memory	512MB DDR PC2700 SDRAM @ 333MHz			
Optical drive	Fixed Internal 24X CD-RW/DVD combo			
Hard Drive	30GB Ultra ATA Hard Drive			
Graphics	64MB DDR ATI MOBILITY			
Modem/NIC	Internal Fax Modem & NIC included			
Battery	96Whr Lithium Ion Battery (12 Cell)			
Operating sytem	Windows XP Home Edition			
Internet access	3 month Sympatica High Speed Internet			
Software	WordPerfect Productivity Pack			
	Computer Systems	1	$ 2,600.00	$ 2,600.00
	GST			$ 130.00
	PST			$ 182.00
	Total			$ 2,912.00

July 3   Bought computer parts and hardware from vendors--Computer Systems Corporation and CompuResource, Inc.

Invoice

Computer Systems Corporation

Purchase Invoice
Invoice No.20996
Sold to: 21st Century Computer Solutions
231 Main Street, Red Deer
AB, T4N 1V6

101 - 3399 #7 Rd.
Richmond, BC V6V 1S7
Customer Order No. 61
Shipped Via
Date Shipped: July 3, 20____
Terms: 2/10, n/30

Quantity		Description	Unit Price	Extended Price
Ordered	Shipped			
5	5	Intel Core 2 Duo E7400 Processor	$ 103.44	$ 517.20
5	5	Intel G31 chipset	$ 151.76	$ 758.80
5	5	2G PC2-5300 2X1GB Memory	$ 24.13	$ 120.65
5	5	250G SATA 11 Hard drive	$ 65.51	$ 327.55
5	5	22x DVD+/-RW Optical drive	$ 20.68	$ 103.40
5	5	410W Power Supply	$ 41.37	$ 206.85
5	5	Windows Vista Business 32bit	$ 82.75	$ 413.75
		Subtotal		$ 2,448.20
		GST		$ 122.41
		PST		Exempt
		Total		$ 2,570.61

CompuResource, Inc.   Purchase Invoice

Unit 9799, 65 Avenue   Invoice No. 1522
Edmonton, AB T6E 0E6

Sold to: 21st Century Computer Solutions   Customer PO # 62
          231 Main Street, Red Deer   Shipped Via:
          AB, T4N 1V6   Date Shipped: July 3, 20____
                                                   Terms: 2/10, n/30

Description	Ordered	Shipped	Price/unit	Extended Price	
23in Samsung Widescreen LCD Monitor	5	5	$ 144.82	$	724.10
Microsoft Efgonomic Keyboard & Mouse set	5	5	$ 36.54	$	182.70
HP P3005 Laser Printer	1	1	$ 510.37	$	510.37
Microsoft Office Professional 2007	3	3	$ 149.97	$	449.91
Microsoft Office 2007 License	1	1	$ 275.86	$	275.86
	Subtotal			$	2,142.94
	GST			$	107.15
	PST				Exempt
	Total			$	2,250.09

July 3   Paid the monthly rent of $1,200 plus GST and PST to Property Management Services. Issued check # 532.

3 Sold 5 computer systems to the Parkland Health Region.

21st CENTURY COMPUTER SOLUTIONS

231 Main Street, Red Deer
AB, T4N 1V6

Sold to: The Parkland Health Region
         6351 Spruce Avenue
         Red Deer, AB T4N 2V6

SALES INVOICE

Invoice No. 100722
Date: July 3, 20____
Customer PO: 50123
Shipped To: Same
Terms: 2/10, n/30

SYSTEM DESCRIPTION				
Reliable Velocity V_BT10001 business system				
Component	**Component Description**	Unit	System Price	Extended Price
Processor	Intel Core 2 Duo E7400 Processor			
Motherboard	Intel G31 chipset			
Graphics	Onboard Graphics			
Memory	2GB PX2-5300 2x1GB Memory			
Hard Drive	250G SATA 11			
Optical Drive	22x DVD+/-RW			
Power Supply	410W			
Operating System	Windows Vista Business 32bit			
Keyboard & Mouse	Microsoft Ergonomic Value Pack			
Software	Microsoft Office 2007 and license			
Monitor	Samsung 23in Widescreen LCD			
	Computer System	5	$ 1,064.07	$ 5,320.35
Printer	HP LaserJet P3005 Laser Printer	1	$ 739.99	$ 739.99
	Subtotal			$ 6,060.34
	GST			$ 303.02
	PST			$ 424.22
	Total			$ 6,787.58

July 4   Received the week's cash deposit sheet and the attached duplicate deposit slip.

*21*ˢᵗ *CENTURY COMPUTER SOLUTIONS*

231 Main Street, Red Deer
Alberta, T4n 1V6

DEPOSIT SHEET   #286   Date: July 4, 20 _____

			Coin		
			Currency	$	2,575.72
			Cheques:		
Cash Allocation:			Mt. Rose School Dist.	$	13,338.00
Computer Sales	$	1,499.75			
Service Fees	$	800.00			
GST	$	114.99			
PST	$	160.98			
	$	2,575.72			
			Total Deposit	$	15,913.72

July 4   Paid the following obligations:

1. Invoice no. 20852 from Computer Systems Corporation less the purchase discount (check # 533).
2. Invoice no. 141 from CompuResource, Inc. net of discount (Check # 534).
3. June accrued salaries: $2,100 for Barry Poor (cheque # 535) and $300.00 for yourself (cheque #536).

July 7   Received computer components and hardware ordered for home computer users from Computer Systems Corporation and CompuResource, Inc.

Invoice

Computer Systems Corporation

Purchase Invoice
Invoice No.21005
Sold to: 21ˢᵗ Century Computer Solutions
          231 Main Street, Red Deer
          AB, T4N 1V6

101 - 3399 #7 Rd.
Richmond, BC V6V 1S7
Customer Order No. 63
Shipped Via
Date Shipped: July 7, 20___
Terms: 2/10, n/30

Quantity Ordered	Shipped	Description	Unit Price	Extended Price
3	3	Intel Core 2 Duo E7400 Processor	$ 103.44	$ 310.32
1	1	AMD Athlon™X2 5200+EE	$ 51.72	$ 51.72
2	2	AMD 780G chipset	$ 121.28	$ 242.56
2	2	Intel G31 chipset	$ 151.76	$ 303.52
4	4	2G PC2-5300 2X1GB Memory	$ 24.13	$ 96.52
4	4	250G SATA 11 Hard drive	$ 65.51	$ 262.04
4	4	22x DVD+/-RW Optical drive	$ 20.68	$ 82.72
4	4	410W Power Supply	$ 41.37	$ 165.48
2	2	Windows Vista Business 32bit	$ 82.75	$ 165.50
2	2	Windows Vista Home Premium 32bit	$ 82.20	$ 164.40
		Subtotal		$ 1,844.78
		GST		$ 92.24
		PST		Exempt
		Total		$ 1,937.02

12

CompuResource, Inc.

Unit 9799, 65 Avenue
Edmonton, AB T6E 0E6

Purchase Invoice

Invoice No. 1890

Sold to: 21st Century Computer Solutions
231 Main Street, Red Deer
AB T4N AB T4N 1V6

Customer PO # 64
Shipped Via:
Date Shipped: July 7, 20___
Terms: 2/10, n/30

Description	Ordered	Shipped	Price/unit	Extended Price
20in Samsung Widescreen LCD Monitor	2	2	134.48	$ 268.96
23in Samsung Widescreen LCD Monitor	2	2	$ 144.82	$ 289.64
Microsoft Efgonomic Keyboard & Mouse set	4	4	$ 36.54	$ 146.16
Microsoft Office Professional 2007	3	3	$ 149.97	$ 449.91
Microsoft Office 2007 License	1	1	$ 275.86	$ 275.86
	Subtotal			$ 1,430.53
	GST			$ 71.53
	PST			Exempt
	Total			$ 1,502.06

July 10 Paid the following invoices: No 10798 from Software Etcetera (cheque no. 537), No. 1522 from CompuResource, Inc. (cheque no. 538) and No. 20996 from Computer systems Corp. (cheque no. 539).

July 14 Received the deposit sheet for the week from Mr. Rich.

*21*st CENTURY COMPUTER SOLUTIONS

231 Main Street, Red Deer
Alberta, T4n 1V6

DEPOSIT SHEET   #287

Date *July 14, 20___*

		Coin		
		Currency	$ 6,731.99	
		Cheques:		
Cash Allocation:		Beautiful Smiles Denture		
Computer Sales	$ 4,466.00	Clinic	$ 4,750.00	
Service Fees	$ 1,200.00	Lakeview University		
GST	$ 444.16	College	$ 2,912.00	
PST	$ 621.83			
	$ 6,731.99			
		Total Deposit	$ 14,393.99	

Patricia A. Ng

July 14   Purchased computer components from Computer Systems Corp.

Invoice

Computer Systems Corporation

Purchase Invoice
Invoice No.21019
 Sold to: 21ˢᵗ Century Computer Solutions
       231 Main Street, Red Deer
       AB, T4N 1V6

101 - 3399 #7 Rd.
Richmond, BC V6V 1S7
Customer Order No <u>65</u>
Shipped Via
Date Shipped: July 14, 20____
Terms: 2/10, n/30

Quantity		Description	Unit Price	Extended Price
Ordered	Shipped			
8	8	Intel™i7 Processor 920	$ 172.48	$ 1,379.84
2	2	AMD Athlon™X2 5200+EE	$ 51.73	$ 103.46
10	10	Intel X58 Chipset	$ 272.41	$ 2,724.10
10	10	ATI FirePro V3750 Professional Graphic Card	$ 137.92	$ 1,379.20
10	10	3x2G 1600MHz DDR3 Memory	$ 85.51	$ 855.10
10	10	500GB 7200RPM SATA	$ 51.72	$ 517.20
10	10	22xDVD+/-RW	$ 20.69	$ 206.90
8	8	All-in-1 card reader	$ 6.89	$ 55.12
10	10	Velocity IW-C583T Mid Tower	$ 75.86	$ 758.60
8	8	460W	$ 62.02	$ 496.16
8	8	Windows Vista Business 64bit	$ 107.65	$ 861.20
2	2	Windows Vista Home Premium 32 bit	$ 82.20	$ 164.40
		Subtotal		$ 9,501.28
		GST		$ 475.06
		PST		Exempt
		Total		$ 9,976.34

14

July 14 Purchased computer system hardware and software from CompuResource, Inc.

CompuResource, Inc.   Purchase Invoice

Unit 9799, 65 Avenue
Edmonton, AB T6E 0E6

Invoice No. 2019

Sold to: 21st Century Computer Solutions
231 Main Street, Red Deer
AB, T4N 1V6

Customer PO # 66
Shipped Via:
Date Shipped: July 14, 20 _____
Terms: 2/10, n/30

Description	Ordered	Shipped	Price/unit	Extended Price
Samsung 24in Widescreen LCD Monitor	10	10	$ 222.50	$ 2,225.00
Microsoft Ergonomic Keyboard & Mouse	10	10	$ 36.54	$ 365.40
HP LaserJet P3005 Laser Printer	5	5	$ 535.58	$ 2,677.90
Microsoft Office Professional 2007	3	3	$ 149.97	$ 449.91
Microsoft office 2007 License	1	1	$ 275.86	$ 275.86
	Subtotal			$ 5,268.30
	GST			$ 263.42
	PST			Exempt
	Total			$ 5,531.72

July 15   Paid the following liabilities:

1.   The excess of the GST payable over the GST paid on purchases as of June 30 to the Receiver General. Issued cheque # 540.

2. The telephone bill with cheque # 541.

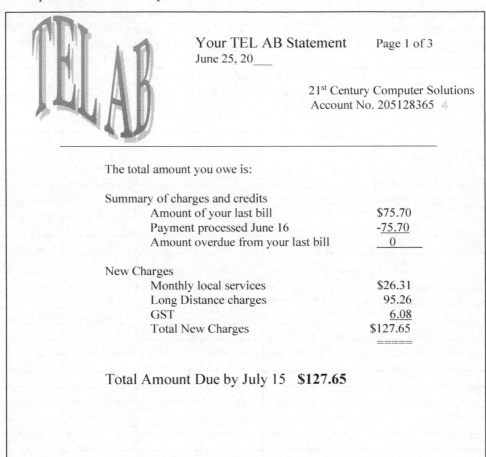

Your TEL AB Statement   Page 1 of 3
June 25, 20___

21st Century Computer Solutions
Account No. 205128365

The total amount you owe is:

Summary of charges and credits
        Amount of your last bill $75.70
        Payment processed June 16   -75.70
        Amount overdue from your last bill   0

New Charges
        Monthly local services $26.31
        Long Distance charges   95.26
        GST   6.08
        Total New Charges $127.65
                                           ======

Total Amount Due by July 15   **$127.65**

July 17   Received this memo from the owner.

INTER-OFFICE MEMO

FROM: Will B. Rich   DATE: July 17, 20____

TO: Bookkeeper   SUBJECT: Promissory Note

Please record the receipt of a 60-day, 10% promissory note from Bountiful Farms in settlement of their account.

July 18   Sold 8 computers to Lakeview University College.

21st CENTURY COMPUTER SOLUTIONS

231 Main Street, Red Deer
AB, T4N 1V6

Sold to: Lakeview University College
      101 Lake Drive
      Centralta, AB T4P 1N5

SALES INVOICE
Invoice No. 100727
Date: July 18, 20_____
Customer PO: 101965
Shipped To: Same
Terms: 2/10, n/30

SYSTEM DESCRIPTION

High Performance Velocity V_BT30101 System

Component	Component Description	unit	System Price	Extended Price
Processor	Intel® Core™ i7 Processor 920			
Motherboard	Intel X58 Chipset			
Graphics	ATI FirePro V3750 Professional Graphic Card			
Memory	3x2G 1600MHz DDR3 Memory			
Hard Drive	500GB 7200RPM SATA			
Optical Drive	22x DVD+/-RW			
Card Reader	All-in-1 card reader			
Chassis	Velocity 1W-C583T Mid Tower			
Power Supply	460W			
Operating System	Windows Vista Business 64bit			
Monitor	23in Widescreen LCD			
Software	Microsoft Office Professional 2007 & License			
Keyboard & mouse	Microsoft Ergonomic Value Pack			
	Computer System	8	$1,815.00	$ 14,520.00
Printer	HP Laser Jet P3005 Laser Printer	2	$ 740.00	$ 1,480.00
	Subtotal			$ 16,000.00
	GST			$ 800.00
	PST			$ 1,120.00
	Total			$ 17,920.00

July 18   Received the following source documents from Mr. Rich.

21_{st} *CENTURY COMPUTER SOLUTIONS*

231 Main Street, Red Deer
Alberta, T4n 1V6

DEPOSIT SHEET   #288   Date: July 18, 20_____

		Coin		
		Currency		$ 1,568.00
		Cheques:		
Cash Allocation:				
Computer Sales				
Service Fees	$ 1,400.00			
GST	$ 70.00			
PST	$ 98.00			
	$ 1,568.00			
		Total Deposit		$ 1,568.00

INTER-OFFICE MEMO

FROM: Will B. Rich   DATE: July 18, 20____

TO: Bookkeeper   SUBJECT: Share of utilities

1. Please issue a cheque to Property Management Services for the company's share of utilities as per attached bill. (Cheque # 542).

Share of utilities	$68.00
GST	3.40
Total	$71.40

2. Please issue a cheque to Barry Poor for $2100.00 (cheque # 543) and to yourself, $300.00 (cheque # 544) for your bi-weekly salaries (Ignore payroll taxes).

July 24   Paid vendors for purchases received on the 7th of the month. (Cheques # 545 & 546).

July 25   The deposit sheet for the week follows.

21st CENTURY COMPUTER SOLUTIONS

231 Main Street, Red Deer
Alberta, T4n 1V6

DEPOSIT SHEET   #289   Date: July 25, 20_____

			Coin	
			Currency	$ 5,519.83
			Cheques:	
Cash Allocation:				
Computer Sales	$	2,871.00		
Service Fees	$	1,900.00		
GST	$	312.01		
PST	$	436.82		
	$	5,519.83		
			Total Deposit	$ 5,519.83

July 26 Bought computer parts and hardware from suppliers.

Invoice

Computer Systems Corporation

Purchase Invoice
Invoice No.21045

101 - 3399 #7 Rd.
Richmond, BC V6V 1S7

Sold to: 21st Century Computer Solutions
231 Main Street, Red Deer
AB, T4N 1V6

Customer Order No. <u>68</u>
Shipped Via
Date Shipped: July 26, 20_____
Terms: 2/10, n/30

| Quantity | | | Unit | Extended |
Ordered	Shipped	Description	Price	Price
3	3	Intel Core i5 2400 processor	$ 182.48	$ 547.44
3	3	DQ67SW Desktop board	$ 241.98	$ 725.94
3	3	2x4GB DDR3 Memory	$ 35.13	$ 105.39
3	3	500GB SATA 11 Hard Drive	$ 65.51	$ 196.53
3	3	CT583T MidTower	$ 79.86	$ 239.58
3	3	22XDVD+/-RW Optical Drive	$ 24.68	$ 74.04
3	3	460W Power Supply	$ 65.02	$ 195.06
2	2	Windows Professional 64 bit	$ 107.65	$ 215.30
1	1	Windows Vista Home Premium 64bit	$ 92.75	$ 92.75
		Subtotal		$ 2,392.03
		GST		$ 119.60
		PST		Exempt
		Total		$ 2,511.63

CompuResource, Inc.　　Purchase Invoice

Unit 9799, 65 Avenue
Edmonton, AB T6E 0E6

Invoice No. 2641

Sold to: 21st Century Computer Solutions	Customer PO # 67
231 Main Street, Red Deer	Shipped Via:
AB, T4N 1V6	Date Shipped: July 26, 20____
	Terms: 2/10, n/30

Description	Ordered	Shipped	Price/unit	Extended
24in widescreen LCD Samsung monitor	2	2	$ 165.00	$ 330.00
21.5in Widescreen LCD LG monitor	1	1	$ 92.96	$ 92.96
Microsoft Ergonomic Keyboard & Mouse	3	3	$ 36.54	$ 109.62
HP LaserJet Laser Printer	2	2	$ 206.89	$ 413.78
Microsoft Office 2007	3	3	$ 114.19	$ 342.57
Subtotal				$ 1,288.93
GST				$ 64.45
PST				Exempt
Total				$ 1,353.38

July 31　Bank deposit for the week.

21st CENTURY COMPUTER SOLUTIONS

231 Main Street, Red Deer
Alberta, T4n 1V6

DEPOSIT SHEET　#230　　　　　　　Date: July 31, 20_____

			Coin	
			Currency	$ 448.00
			Cheques:	
Cash Allocation:			Parkland Health Region	$6,787.58
Computer Sales				
Service Fees	$ 400.00			
GST	$ 20.00			
PST	$ 28.00			
	$ 448.00			
			Total Deposit	$ 7,235.58

July 31   Sold 2 computer systems to Weir, Allgood & Albright, Barristers and Solicitors.

21*st* CENTURY COMPUTER SOLUTIONS

231 Main Street, Red Deer
AB, T4N 1V6

SALES INVOICE
Invoice No. 100732
Date: July 31, 20___

Sold to: Weir, Allgood, & Albright, Barristers and Solicitors
          #5 68951 Professional Center
          Riverside St., Lacombe, AB T4l 1P7

Customer PO:
Shipped To: Same
Terms: 2/10, n/30

SYSTEM DESCRIPTION				
Reliable Velocity BT 20201 Business System.				
Component	**Component Description**	Unit	System Price	Extended Price
Processor	Intel Core i5 2400 Processor			
Motherboard	DQ67SW Desktop board			
Memory	2x4GB DDR3 Memory			
Hard Drive	500GB SATA 11			
Optical Drive	22z DVD+/-RW			
Power Supply	460W			
Operating System	Windows 7 Professional 64bit			
Monitor	Samsung 24in Widescreen LCD with DVI			
Keyboare & mouse	Microsoft Ergonomic Value Pack			
Software	Microsoft Office 2007			
	Computer Systems	2	$ 1,775.00	$ 3,550.00
Printer	HP Laser Jet Printer	1	$ 270.00	$ 270.00
	Subtotal			$ 3,820.00
	GST			$ 191.00
	PST			$ 267.40
	Total			$ 4,278.40

July 31 Received this memorandum from Mr. Rich.

INTER-OFFICE MEMO

FROM: Will B. Rich   DATE: July 31, 20_____

TO: Bookkeeper.   SUBJECT: Petty Cash, etc.

---

1.   The following is a summary of petty cash expenses as per attached receipts. Please issue cheque #547 to replenish the fund.

GST	$ 7.02
Transportation in	79.35
Delivery Expense	61.00
Total	$147.37

2.   Please issue a cheque to me for $2,500 and charge it to my drawing account (cheque # 548).

3.   Adjust the CompuResource, Inc. account for software damaged in transit, $61.06. This amount includes GST of $2.91.

4.   Please adjust the accounts affected by the following transactions and events. (**N.B. If using the manual version, complete the following adjustments as part of instruction number 3, c.)**

   a.   Depreciation for the month: Office Furniture &Equipment, $60; Motor Vehicles, $1,079.20.

   b.   Expired insurance, $121.

   c.   Accrued salaries, $2,400.00.

   d.   Office supplies on hand, $420.00; computer supplies on hand, $398.00.

   e.   Inventory on hand, $1,246.12. (Manual Version—use this information to complete the worksheet.)

Patricia A. Ng

CBofC Chartered Bank of Canada

32 Riverside Ave., Red Deer
Alberta, T4N 1R7

Account No. 01-98765

21st Century Computer Solutions

the Month Ended July 31, 20_____   31 Main Street, Red Deer, Alberta, T4N 1V6

Date	Description	Debit	Credit	Balance
June 30	Balance Forward			$ 28,056.21
July 1	Automatic Deduction: Monthly loan payment	933.33		27,122.88
1	Cheque 498	10,238.00		16,884.88
1	Deposit		5,365.25	22,250.13
6	Cheque 530	310.00		21,940.13
8	Deposit		15,913.72	37,853.85
9	Cheque 532	1,344.00		36,509.85
10	Cheque 535	2,100.00		34,409.85
	Cheque 536	300.00		34,109.85
15	Cheque 533	14,251.28		19,858.57
	Deposit		14,393.99	34,252.56
17	Cheque 534	894.63		33,357.93
19	Cheque 538	2,207.23		31,150.70
22	Cheque 543	2,100.00		29,050.70
	Deposit		1,568.00	30,618.70
	Cheque 544	300.00		30,318.70
23	Cheque 537	515.00		29,803.70
26	Cheque 541	127.65		29,676.05
	Cheque 542	71.40		29,604.65
	Cheque 539	2,521.65		27,083.00
	Cheque 540	1,820.00		25,263.00
	Cheque 545	1,937.02		23,325.98
26	Deposit		5,519.83	28,845.81
29	Bank Service Charge	30.10		28,815.71

21st Century Computer Solutions			
Bank Reconciliation			
June 30, 20_____			
Balance per Bank	28,056.21	Balance per Books	22,908.66
Add:			
Deposit of June 28	5,365.25		
	33,421.46		
Deduct:		Deduct:	
Outstanding cheques:		Bank Service Charge	35.20
No. 530	310.00		
No. 498	10,238.00		
	10,548.00		
Reconciled Balance	22,873.46	Reconciled Balance	22,873.46

21st Century Computer Solutions			
Bank Reconciliation			
July 31, 20_____			

Journals

Special Journals

- Sales Journal
- Purchases Journal
- Cash Receipts Journal
- Cash Disbursements Journal

General Journal

Sales Journal

Page 3

Date	Account Debited	Post. Ref.	Invoice No.	Accts. Rec'ble Debit	Computer Sales Credit	GST Payable Credit	PST Payable Credit

Purchases Journal

Page 5

Date	Account Credited	P.R.	Terms	Invoice No.	Purchases Debit	GST Payable Debit	Accounts Payable Credit

Patricia A. Ng

Cash Receipts Journal

Page 3

Date	Explanation or Account Credited	Post. Ref.	Cash Debit	Acct. Receivable Credit	Computer Sales Credit	Sales Discount Debit	Service Fees Credit	GST Payable Credit	PST Payable Credit

Cash Disbursements Journal

Date	Description or Account Debited/Credited	Cheque No.	P. R.	Accts. Payable Debit	Other Accts. Debit	Other Accts. Credit	Purchase Disc. Credit	GST Payable Debit	Cash Credit

		General Journal			Page 7	
Date		Account Titles and Explanation	Post. Ref.	Debit	Credit	

Date	Account Titles and Explanation	Post. Ref.	Debit	Credit

General Journal — Page 8

Ledgers

- General Ledger
- Accounts Receivable Subsidiary Ledger
- Accounts Payable Subsidiary Ledger

GENERAL LEDGER

Account: Cash   Account No. 1010

Date		Explanation	P. R.	Debit		Credit		Balance	
June	30	Balance						22 873	46

Account: Petty Cash   Account No. 1030

Date		Explanation	P. R.	Debit		Credit		Balance	
June	30	Balance						250	00

Account: Accounts Receivable   Account No. 1050

Date		Explanation	P. R.	Debit		Credit		Balance	
June	30	Balance						20 208	00

Account: Allowance for Doubtful Accounts   Account No. 1060

Date		Explanation	P. R.	Debit		Credit		Balance	
June	30	Balance						101	00

Account: Notes Receivable					Account No. 1110			
Date		Explanation	P. R.	Debit		Credit		Balance

Account: Inventory					Account No. 1120			
Date		Explanation	P. R.	Debit		Credit		Balance
June	30	Balance						3 060 24

Account: Computer Supplies					Acount No. 1150			
Date		Explanation	P. R.	Debit		Credit		Balance
June	30	Balance						749 00

Account:Office Supplies					Account No. 1190			
Date		Explanation	P. R.	Debit		Credit		Balance
June	30	Balance						625 00

Account: Prepaid Insurance					Account No. 1210			
Date		Explanation	P. R.	Debit		Credit		Balance
June	30	Balance						726 00

Account: Office Furniture & Equipment Account No. 1510

Date		Explanation	P. R.	Debit		Credit		Balance		
June	30	Balance						19	650	25

Account: Accumulated Depreciation-Office Furniture & Equipment Account No. 1520

Date		Explanation	P. R.	Debit		Credit		Balance		
June	30	Balance						6	163	00

Account: Motor Vehicle Account No. 1560

Date		Explanation	P. R.	Debit		Credit		Balance		
June	30	Balance						48	850	00

Account: Accumulated Depreciation - Motor Vehicle Account No. 1570

Date		Explanation	P. R.	Debit		Credit		Balance		
June	30	Balance						5	682	00

Account: Accounts Payable Account No. 2010

Date		Explanation	P. R.	Debit		Credit		Balance		
June	30	Balance						15	955	00

Patricia A. Ng

Account: GST Payable				Account No. 2110						
Date		Explanation	P. R.	Debit			Credit		Balance	
June	30	Balance							1 820	00

Account: PST Payable				Account No. 2130						
Date		Explanation	P. R.	Debit			Credit		Balance	
June	30	Balance							2 989	00

Account: Salaries Payable				Account No. 2150						
Date		Explanation	P. R.	Debit			Credit		Balance	
June	30	Balance							2	400 00

Account: Development Bank Loan Payable				Account No. 2550							
Date		Explanation	P. R.	Debit		Credit		Balance			
June	30	Balance						10	150	25	

Account: Will B. Rich, Capital				Account No. 3010							
Date		Explanation	P. R.	Debit		Credit		Balance			
June	30	Balance						71	731	70	

Account: Will B. Rich, Drawing				Account No. 3020							
Date		Explanation	P. R.	Debit		Credit		Balance			

Account: Computer Sales				Account No. 4010							
Date		Explanation	P. R.	Debit		Credit		Balance			

Account: Sales Discount				Account No. 4011							
Date		Explanation	P. R.	Debit		Credit		Balance			

Account: Service Fees				Account No. 4050		
Date	Explanation	P. R.	Debit	Credit	Balance

Account: Purchases				Account No. 5010		
Date	Explanation	P. R.	Debit	Credit	Balance

Account: Purchase Returns & Allowances				Account No. 5020		
Date	Explanation	P. R.	Debit	Credit	Balance

Account: Purchase Discount				Account No. 5030		
Date	Explanation	P. R.	Debit	Credit	Balance

Account: Transportation In				Account No. 5040		
Date	Explanation	P. R.	Debit	Credit	Balance

Account: Depreciation Expense-Office Furniture & Equipment			Account No. 5605							
Date		Explanation	P. R.	Debit			Credit		Balance	

Account: Depreciation Expense-Motor Vehicle			Account No. 5611							
Date		Explanation	P. R.	Debit			Credit		Balance	

Account: Delivery Expense			Account No. 5615							
Date		Explanation	P. R.	Debit			Credit		Balance	

Account: Insurance Expense			Account No. 5617							
Date		Explanation	P. R.	Debit			Credit		Balance	

Account: Interest Expense			Account No. 5619							
Date		Explanation	P. R.	Debit			Credit		Balance	

Account: Salaries Expense				Account No. 5621		
Date		Explanation	P. R.	Debit	Credit	Balance

Account: Computer Supplies Expense				Account No. 5629		
Date		Explanation	P. R.	Debit	Credit	Balance

Account: Office Supplies Expense				Account No. 5630		
Date		Explanation	P. R.	Debit	Credit	Balance

Account: Bad Debt Expense				Account No. 5632		
Date		Explanation	P. R.	Debit	Credit	Balance

Account: Rent Expense				Account No. 5633		
Date		Explanation	P. R.	Debit	Credit	Balance

Account: Telephone Expense   Account No. 5635

Date	Explanation	P. R.	Debit	Credit	Balance

Account: Utilities Expense   Account No. 5637

Date	Explanation	P. R.	Debit	Credit	Balance

Account: Miscellaneous Expense   Account No. 5640

Date	Explanation	P. R.	Debit	Credit	Balance

Account: Income Summary   Account No. 9999

Date	Explanation	P. R.	Debit	Credit	Balance

Account:

Date	Explanation	P. R.	Debit	Credit	Balance

ACCOUNTS RECEIVABLE SUBSIDIARY LEDGER

Account: Beautiful Smiles Denture Clinic

Date		Explanation	P. R.	Debit	Credit	Balance
June	30	Balance				4 750 00

Account: Bountiful Farms

Date		Explanation	P. R.	Debit	Credit	Balance
June	30	Balance				2 120 00

Account: Lakeview University College

Date		Explanation	P. R.	Debit	Credit	Balance

Mount Rose School District

Date		Explanation	P. R.	Debit	Credit	Balance
June	30	Balance				13 338 00

Account: Parkland Health Region													
Date		Explanation	P. R.	Debit			Credit			Balance			

Account: Weir, Allgood & Albright, Barristers & Solicitors													
Date		Explanation	P. R.	Debit			Credit			Balance			

ACCOUNTS PAYABLE SUBSIDIARY LEDGER

Account: CompuResource, Inc.

Date		Explanation	P. R.	Debit		Credit		Balance	
June	30	Balance						912	00

Account: Computer Systems Corporation

Date		Explanation	P. R.	Debit		Credit		Balance		
June	30	Balance						14	528	00

Account: Software, Etcetera

Date		Explanation	P. R.	Debit		Credit		Balance	
June	30	Balance						515	00

Accounting Forms

- Worksheet
- 3-column accounting sheet
- Post-Closing Trial Balance Form
- Schedule of Accounts Receivable Form
- Schedule of Accounts Payable Form

21st Century Computer Solutions
Worksheet

Account Titles	Unadjusted Trial Balance		Adjustments		Adjusted Trial Balance		Income Statement		Balance Sheet	
	Debit	Credit	Debit	Credit	Debit	Credit	Debit	Credit	Debit	Credit

21st Century Computer Solutions		
Post-Closing Trial Balance		
July 31, 20_____		

21st Century Computer Solutions		
Schedule of Accounts Receivable		
July 31, 20_____		

21st Century Computer Solutions		
Schedule of Accounts Payable		
July 31, 20_____		

Cheque Book

No. 532 $_____

Date _____ 20___

Pay to _____

For _____

	Dollars	Cents
Bal Bro't For'd	22,873	46
Deposits(Add)		
Charges(Subtract)		
Subtotal		
This Cheque		
Bal Car'd For'd		

21st Century Computer Solutions   532
231 Main Street, Red Deer
Alberta, T4N 1V6   Date _____ 20 ____

PAY TO THE

ORDER OF _____ $_____

_____ /100 DOLLARS

CHARTERED BANK OF CANADA
132 Riverside Ave., Red Deer
Alberta, T4N 1R7

For _____ _____

‖‎532‖ : 01234‖.432: 01‖98765‖

No. 533 $_____

Date _____ 20___

Pay to _____

For _____

	Dollars	Cents
Bal Bro't For'd		
Deposits(Add)		
Charges(Subtract)		
Subtotal		
This Cheque		
Bal Car'd For'd		

21st Century Computer Solutions   533
231 Main Street, Red Deer
Alberta, T4N 1V6   Date _____ 20 ____

PAY TO THE

ORDER OF _____ $_____

_____ /100 DOLLARS

CHARTERED BANK OF CANADA
132 Riverside Ave., Red Deer
Alberta, T4N 1R7

For _____ _____

‖‎533‖ : 01234‖.432: 01‖98765‖

No. 534 $_____

Date _____ 20___

Pay to _____

For _____

	Dollars	Cents
Bal Bro't For'd		
Deposits(Add)		
Charges(Subtract)		
Subtotal		
This Cheque		
Bal Car'd For'd		

21st Century Computer Solutions   534
231 Main Street, Red Deer
Alberta, T4N 1V6   Date July 4 ____ 20 ____

PAY TO THE

ORDER OF *Compuresource, Inc.* $*894.63*

Eight hundred ninety-four and _____ 63/100 DOLLARS

CHARTERED BANK OF CANADA
132 Riverside Ave., Red Deer
Alberta, T4N 1R7

For _____ _____

‖‎534‖ : 01234‖.432: 01‖98765‖

No. 535 $_____ | 21st Century Computer Solutions   535

Date _____ 20___ | 231 Main Street, Red Deer

Pay to _____ | Alberta, T4N 1V6   Date _____ 20____

For _____ |

  | PAY TO THE

_____ | ORDER OF _____ $_____

|Dollars |Cents|

Bal Bro't For'd   ___|___ | _____ /100 DOLLARS

Deposits (Add)   ___|___ |

Charges (Subtract) ___|___   CHARTERED BANK OF CANADA

Subtotal   ___|___   132 Riverside Ave., Red Deer

This Cheque   ___|___   Alberta, T4N 1R7

Bal Car'd For'd   ___|___   For _____ _____

  ||'535|| : 01234||.432: 01||98765||

No. 536 $_____ | 21st Century Computer Solutions   536

Date _____ 20___ | 231 Main Street, Red Deer

Pay to _____ | Alberta, T4N 1V6   Date _____ 20____

For _____ |

  | PAY TO THE

_____ | ORDER OF _____ $_____

|Dollars |Cents|

Bal Bro't For'd   ___|___ | _____ /100 DOLLARS

Deposits (Add)   ___|___ |

Charges (Subtract) ___|___ | CHARTERED BANK OF CANADA

Subtotal   ___|___ | 132 Riverside Ave., Red Deer

This Cheque   ___|___ | Alberta, T4N 1R7

Bal Car'd For'd   ___|___ | For _____ _____

  ||'536|| : 01234||.432: 01||98765||

No. 537 $_____ | 21st Century Computer Solutions   537

Date _____ 20___ | 231 Main Street, Red Deer

Pay to _____ | Alberta, T4N 1V6   Date _____ 20____

For _____ |

  | PAY TO THE

_____ | ORDER OF _____ $_____

|Dollars |Cents|

Bal Bro't For'd   ___|___ | _____ /100 DOLLARS

Deposits (Add)   ___|___ |

Charges (Subtract) ___|___ | CHARTERED BANK OF CANADA

Subtotal   ___|___ | 132 Riverside Ave., Red Deer

This Cheque   ___|___ | Alberta, T4N 1R7

Bal Car'd For'd   ___|___ | For _____ _____

  ||'537|| : 01234||.432: 01||98765||

No. 538 $_____

Date _____ 20___

Pay to _____

For _____

	Dollars	Cents
Bal Bro't For'd		
Deposits (Add)		
Charges (Subtract)		
Subtotal		
This Cheque		
Bal Car'd For'd		

21st Century Computer Solutions   538

231 Main Street, Red Deer

Alberta, T4N 1V6   Date _____ 20____

PAY TO THE

ORDER OF _____ $_____

_____ /100 DOLLARS

CHARTERED BANK OF CANADA

132 Riverside Ave., Red Deer

Alberta, T4N 1R7

For _____

||'538|| : 01234||.432: 01||98765||

No. 539 $_____

Date _____ 20___

Pay to _____

For _____

	Dollars	Cents
Bal Bro't For'd		
Deposits (Add)		
Charges (Subtract)		
Subtotal		
This Cheque		
Bal Car'd For'd		

21st Century Computer Solutions   539

231 Main Street, Red Deer

Alberta, T4N 1V6   Date _____ 20____

PAY TO THE

ORDER OF _____ $_____

_____ /100 DOLLARS

CHARTERED BANK OF CANADA

132 Riverside Ave., Red Deer

Alberta, T4N 1R7

For _____

||'539|| : 01234||.432: 01||98765||

No. 540 $_____

Date _____ 20___

Pay to _____

For _____

	Dollars	Cents
Bal Bro't For'd		
Deposits (Add)		
Charges (Subtract)		
Subtotal		
This Cheque		
Bal Car'd For'd		

21st Century Computer Solutions   540

231 Main Street, Red Deer

Alberta, T4N 1V6   Date _____ 20____

PAY TO THE

ORDER OF *The Receiver General*   *$ 1,820.00*

One thousand, eight hundred twenty only /100 DOLLARS

CHARTERED BANK OF CANADA

132 Riverside Ave., Red Deer

Alberta, T4N 1R7

For _____

||'540|| : 01234||.432: 01||98765||

No. 541	$ _____		21st Century Computer Solutions		541
Date _____ 20 ___			231 Main Street, Red Deer		
Pay to _____			Alberta, T4N 1V6	Date _____ 20 ___	
For _____					

PAY TO THE
ORDER OF _____ $ _____

_____ /100 DOLLARS

	Dollars	Cents
Bal Bro't For'd	_____	_____
Deposits (Add)	_____	_____
Charges (Subtract)	_____	_____
Subtotal	_____	_____
This Cheque	_____	_____
Bal Car'd For'd	_____	_____

CHARTERED BANK OF CANADA
132 Riverside Ave., Red Deer
Alberta, T4N 1R7
For _____ _____

||˙541|| : 01234||.432: 01||98765||

No. 542	$ _____		21st Century Computer Solutions		542
Date _____ 20 ___			231 Main Street, Red Deer		
Pay to _____			Alberta, T4N 1V6	Date _____ 20 ___	
For _____					

PAY TO THE
ORDER OF _____ $ _____

_____ /100 DOLLARS

	Dollars	Cents
Bal Bro't For'd	_____	_____
Deposits (Add)	_____	_____
Charges (Subtract)	_____	_____
Subtotal	_____	_____
This Cheque	_____	_____
Bal Car'd For'd	_____	_____

CHARTERED BANK OF CANADA
132 Riverside Ave., Red Deer
Alberta, T4N 1R7
For _____ _____

||˙542|| : 01234||.432: 01||98765||

No. 543	$ _____		21st Century Computer Solutions		543
Date _____ 20 ___			231 Main Street, Red Deer		
Pay to _____			Alberta, T4N 1V6	Date _____ 20 ___	
For _____					

PAY TO THE
ORDER OF _____ $ _____

_____ /100 DOLLARS

	Dollars	Cents
Bal Bro't For'd	_____	_____
Deposits (Add)	_____	_____
Charges (Subtract)	_____	_____
Subtotal	_____	_____
This Cheque	_____	_____
Bal Car'd For'd	_____	_____

CHARTERED BANK OF CANADA
132 Riverside Ave., Red Deer
Alberta, T4N 1R7
For _____ _____

||˙543|| : 01234||.432: 01||98765||

No. 544 $_____

Date _____20___

Pay to _____

For _____

	Dollars	Cents
Bal Bro't For'd		
Deposits(Add)		
Charges(Subtract)		
Subtotal		
This Cheque		
Bal Car'd For'd		

21st Century Computer Solutions   544

231 Main Street, Red Deer

Alberta, T4N 1V6   Date _____20____

PAY TO THE

ORDER OF _____$_____

_____/100 DOLLARS

CHARTERED BANK OF CANADA

132 Riverside Ave., Red Deer

Alberta, T4N 1R7

For _____ _____

||'544|| : 01234||.432: 01||98765||

No. 545 $_____

Date _____20___

Pay to _____

For _____

	Dollars	Cents
Bal Bro't For'd		
Deposits(Add)		
Charges(Subtract)		
Subtotal		
This Cheque		
Bal Car'd For'd		

21st Century Computer Solutions   545

231 Main Street, Red Deer

Alberta, T4N 1V6   Date _____20____

PAY TO THE

ORDER OF _____$_____

_____/100 DOLLARS

CHARTERED BANK OF CANADA

132 Riverside Ave., Red Deer

Alberta, T4N 1R7

For _____ _____

||'545|| : 01234||.432: 01||98765||

No. 546 $_____

Date _____20___

Pay to _____

For _____

	Dollars	Cents
Bal Bro't For'd		
Deposits(Add)		
Charges(Subtract)		
Subtotal		
This Cheque		
Bal Car'd For'd		

21st Century Computer Solutions   546

231 Main Street, Red Deer

Alberta, T4N 1V6   Date _____20____

PAY TO THE

ORDER OF _____$_____

_____/100 DOLLARS

CHARTERED BANK OF CANADA

132 Riverside Ave., Red Deer

Alberta, T4N 1R7

For _____ _____

||'546|| : 01234||.432: 01||98765||

No. 547	$_____		21st Century Computer Solutions		547
Date _____ 20___			231 Main Street, Red Deer		
Pay to _____			Alberta, T4N 1V6	Date _____ 20____	
For _____					

PAY TO THE
ORDER OF _____ $_____

	Dollars	Cents
Bal Bro't For'd	_____	_____
Deposits (Add)	_____	_____
Charges (Subtract)	_____	_____
Subtotal	_____	_____
This Cheque	_____	_____
Bal Car'd For'd	_____	_____

_____ /100 DOLLARS

CHARTERED BANK OF CANADA
132 Riverside Ave., Red Deer
Alberta, T4N 1R7
For _____ _____

||'547|| : 01234||.432: 01||98765||

No. 548	$_____		21st Century Computer Solutions		548
Date _____ 20___			231 Main Street, Red Deer		
Pay to _____			Alberta, T4N 1V6	Date _____ 20____	
For _____					

PAY TO THE
ORDER OF _____ $_____

	Dollars	Cents
Bal Bro't For'd	_____	_____
Deposits (Add)	_____	_____
Charges (Subtract)	_____	_____
Subtotal	_____	_____
This Cheque	_____	_____
Bal Car'd For'd	_____	_____

_____ /100 DOLLARS

CHARTERED BANK OF CANADA
132 Riverside Ave., Red Deer
Alberta, T4N 1R7
For _____ _____

||'548|| : 01234||.432: 01||98765||

No. 549	$_____		21st Century Computer Solutions		549
Date _____ 20___			231 Main Street, Red Deer		
Pay to _____			Alberta, T4N 1V6	Date _____ 20____	
For _____					

PAY TO THE
ORDER OF _____ $_____

	Dollars	Cents
Bal Bro't For'd	_____	_____
Deposits (Add)	_____	_____
Charges (Subtract)	_____	_____
Subtotal	_____	_____
This Cheque	_____	_____
Bal Car'd For'd	_____	_____

_____ /100 DOLLARS

CHARTERED BANK OF CANADA
132 Riverside Ave., Red Deer
Alberta, T4N 1R7
For _____ _____

||'549|| : 01234||.432: 01||98765||

No. 550	$
Date	20
Pay to	
For	

	Dollars	Cents
Bal Bro't For'd		
Deposits (Add)		
Charges (Subtract)		
Subtotal		
This Cheque		
Bal Car'd For'd		

21st Century Computer Solutions   550
231 Main Street, Red Deer
Alberta, T4N 1V6   Date _____ 20____

PAY TO THE
ORDER OF _____ $_____

_____ /100 DOLLARS

CHARTERED BANK OF CANADA
132 Riverside Ave., Red Deer
Alberta, T4N 1R7
For _____

||'550|| : 01234||.432: 01||98765||

No. 551	$
Date	20
Pay to	
For	

	Dollars	Cents
Bal Bro't For'd		
Deposits (Add)		
Charges (Subtract)		
Subtotal		
This Cheque		
Bal Car'd For'd		

21st Century Computer Solutions   551
231 Main Street, Red Deer
Alberta, T4N 1V6   Date _____ 20____

PAY TO THE
ORDER OF _____ $_____

_____ /100 DOLLARS

CHARTERED BANK OF CANADA
132 Riverside Ave., Red Deer
Alberta, T4N 1R7
For _____

||'551|| : 01234||.432: 01||98765||

Give a man a fish and you feed him for a day.
Teach a man to fish and you feed him for a lifetime.
Chinese Proverb.